Charismatic Control

The

Witchcraft

of

Domination and Control

in

Neo-Pentecostal Churches

by
Steven Lambert, ThD

Unless otherwise indicated, all Scripture quotations are taken from the NEW AMERICAN STANDARD BIBLE, © Copyright 1960, 1962, 1963, 1968, 1971, 1972, 1973, 1975, 1977, 1988, The Lockman Foundation. Used by permission.

Emphasis and explanations added by the author in certain Scripture citings appear within parentheses or brackets.

This booklet is adapted from a book by the same author, *Charismatic Captivation* (ISBN 9781887915007).

Charismatic Control
ISBN 978-1-887915-01-4

© Copyright 1997; Steven Lambert, ThD, DMin. All rights reserved under International Copyright Law. Contents and/or cover may not be reproduced in whole or in part in any form without the express written consent of the author. Author website: http://www.slm.org.

Published by:
Real Truth Publications
PO Box 911
Jupiter FL 33468
E-Mail: editor@realtruthpublications.com
Website: http://www.realtruthpublications.com

Printed in the United States of America

Table of Contents

Chapter 1: Problem and Premise
Chapter 2: Religious Enslavement: Sorcery
Chapter 3: The Signs of Authoritarian Abuse & Common Control Mechanisms

---

For there are many rebellious men, empty talkers and deceivers who must be silenced because they are upsetting whole families, teaching things they should not teach, for the sake of sordid gain....for this cause reprove them severely that they may be sound in the faith not paying attention to...myths and commandments of men who turn away from the truth. To the pure all things are pure; but to those who are perverted and unbelieving, nothing is pure, but both their mind and their conscience are perverted. They profess to know God, but by their deeds they deny him, being detestable and disobedient, and worthless for any good deed. But as for you, speak the things which are fitting for sound doctrine. — **Titus 1:10-2:1**

This booklet is adapted from Dr. Lambert's book, *Charismatic Captivation*, which contains a wealth of information regarding the prevalent problem of hyper-authoritarianism in Neo-Pentecostal churches, how it began, why it is improper, and how to recognize and be set free from it. Readers are strongly encouraged to obtain a copy of that book for a more detailed account of this alarmingly widespread and extremely harmful problem. A synopsis, sample chapters, many excerpts of the book, and online ordering are available at: http://www.charismatic-captivation.com.

Chapter One
Problem and Premise

Multitudes of sincere and trusting believers are caught in the virtually invisible web of religious captivation in Charismatic and other Neo-Pentecostal churches, and don't know it. They are unaware victims of spiritual abuse and exploitation perpetrated under the heavy-hand of hyper-authoritarianism. That is to say, the leadership of the church-group of which they are a part is dominating, controlling, and manipulating their followers, thereby exploiting them for personal gain and private kingdom-building.

Horror stories of authoritarian abuse and exploitation and psychological enslavement in bona fide Christian churches abound. From time to time, particular isolated incidents have erupted in highly publicized news stories. However, those high-profile cases are really only the tip of the iceberg. The truth of the matter is, as several decades of my counseling ministry to hundreds of victims bears out, ecclesiastical enslavement and exploitation is widespread in certain sectors of Christendom in this nation. And, it is vital to understand, I'm *not* talking about radical, fringe religious sects and cults, but well-respected church-groups espousing otherwise orthodox Christian beliefs, whose membership is comprised of a cross section of average Americans, individuals and families, of every race, education level, station, and walk of life.

Though religious predomination is certainly nothing new, and hyper-authoritarianism is by no means limited to the Neo-Pentecostal branch of the Church, it has, however, especially flourished in the Charismatic and so-called "second, third, and fourth wave" (i.e., Neo-Pentecostal) groups since it was infused into the very fabric, foundation, and functions of that branch of the Church in the early- to mid-seventies. Moreover, it is the Charismatic branch of which this ministry has been a part since its inception, which gives me not only the "right" but also the duty to bring reproof of error and errancy in that realm (2 Tim. 4:1-5, et al.).

This kind of "Charismatic captivation" is prevalent among Charismatic and other Neo-Pentecostal churches and groups primarily as a result of widely-taught and -accepted hyper-authoritarian doctrines and practices first introduced in the 1970s by an alliance of five ministers who rose to prominence, and spawned what became known as the "Discipleship/Shepherding Movement." Those doctrines and practices remain an integral part of the governmental foundation of many churches and groups yet today.

This elite ministerial Quintumverate had somehow concluded that the newly-created and burgeoning branch of the Church, generated by the Divinely-orchestrated Charismatic Movement, birthed in 1960, was in disarray and needed to be "organized." Somehow they also determined it was they God had appointed to accomplish the task of "organizing" the Charismatic church. The purportedly inspired and Bible-based organizational structure they advocated and eventually instituted was virtually identical to the modern pyramid marketing structure so popular and prevalent today. The "Fab Five" placed themselves at the top of the pyramid of interrelated Charismatic leaders, which quickly expanded into a "downline" of thousands of "submitted" ministers.

In the mid-1970s the entire matter of this "movement" erupted into a highly publicized international controversy. The result of the maelstrom was that the relevant doctrines and practices were repudiated and denounced by many well-known church leaders, and the ministers who invented and promulgated them fell into disrepute.

However, despite the controversy and the public chastisement, those ministers and their followers initially remained unbowed and undeterred. They defended themselves, as well as the hyper-authoritarian teachings and practices and philosophies of church-government they advocated. For many years afterward, they continued to teach those patently false and unscriptural doctrines, and to develop what came to be an expansive multi-level "network" of ministers and churches. Though, it was now done less overtly, and there was a concerted and deliberate effort to take the whole matter underground to lessen as much as possible the negative effects of the controversy and to give the appearance of repentance.

The unfortunate consequence of that move toward covertness and esotericism was that instead of being eradicated, those patently false doctrines and scripturally-prohibited practices were infused into the very fabric and foundation of the Charismatic/Neo-Pentecostal Church at large, and are still espoused and practiced by many churches and groups in operation today. This stems partly from the fact that many of those ministries are headed by leaders who were a part of that network, and adopted or adapted many of the doctrines and governmental philosophies advocated by its principals.

Many church leaders themselves do not realize their leadership methodology is actually a hybrid form of hyper-authoritarianism, and amounts to domination and control. The proper role of human under-shepherds is to lead people to the Great Shepherd, Jesus Christ, and teach them how to be His followers, in submission to *Him* and *His* authority. Hyper-authoritarian leaders, instead, lead people to *themselves*, and indoctrinate them to be their followers, in total submission to them and their authority.

In essence, these dominating shepherds teach they are the church members' Lord, Master, and Savior. They indoctrinate congregants to believe the spiritual leaders of the church themselves are the members' "spiritual covering," and any member who ever leaves the church will be "out from under" their "covering," be without any covering, and experience terrible curses and consequences as a result. This false hypothesis of "absolute submission," with which subjects are incessantly indoctrinated, is the bedrock of such authoritarian doctrines. That, coupled with the enslaving organizational authority structure in place in the groups where these unbiblical doctrines are espoused, is primarily what makes these techniques and mechanisms effectual and effective. And, it is chiefly the spiritual and psychological needs and problems of attendees of these groups that makes them vulnerable to such unauthorized domination and control as well as exploitation.

The mechanisms of psychological manipulation, domination, and control employed in these groups are virtually identical, to those employed by certified cults. Indeed, the stark truth is that many of the groups and churches who employ these techniques and mechanisms are themselves at the very minimum quasi-cults, and in some cases, bona fide cults.

The abuse and exploitation occurring in groups where these hyper-authoritarian systems of governance are instituted come in various shapes and shades. In a nutshell, the "dumb sheep" are taught they cannot trust their own judgment or ability to receive direction from the Lord for even the most mundane decisions of their lives, but must rely instead upon the supposed transcendent wisdom and superior spirituality of their human "Shepherds." Typically, subjects must obtain the approval of their group-gurus regarding virtually all domestic matters and decisions; matters of romance, such as who members date and marry; health and insurance matters, employment and career matters, and most of all, regarding every detail of members' personal finances, which requires their leaders' approval for practically every significant expenditure.

Relentless programming with this premise along with constant bombardment with belittling derision leads to spiritual and psychological paralysis for submissive adherents. Gradually, as the hidden web of religious witchcraft is woven, and their natural resistance to such domination and control is dissipated, docile subjects eventually become the unwitting and helpless psychological slaves of self-aggrandizing church leaders and their grandiose plans for the building of their private, personal, earthly kingdoms.

In these groups, the "authority" of the "shepherds" is absolute, sacrosanct, and inviolable, that is, without reprisal. Any semblance of anything other than total and unquestioning obeisance to the desires and counsel of the chain of leaders is considered rebellion and insubordination, and simply is not tolerated. Members live under the constant threat of being branded with the Scarlet Letter "R" for "rebel," openly denounced and shamed from the (bully-)pulpit, and consequently shunned by their "covenant-community" as well as the threat of excommunication (which is rarely exercised except in the case of the most outspoken dissidents, because they don't want to lose the members and their financial support).

Moreover, members are indoctrinated to accept the leadership-set agenda and mission of the group, regarding which they have little real say, as their personal burden and responsibility, and to commit their time, talent, and, most importantly, their *tithe* to its successful completion.

The oppressive maltreatment and mistreatment to which members of these cult-like groups are subjected seems to me to be the spiritual equivalent of the hard-taskmastery over the Israelites during their centuries of captivity under the Egyptian Pharaohs.

So what are the consequences and effects we are talking about here, a scant few slightly disillusioned people with their feelings a little hurt? **FAR FROM IT!** We are talking about an immense number of broken and destroyed families, marriages, and friendships, multitudes of unpretentious, formerly trusting people who are now psychologically traumatized and marred, and spiritually shipwrecked, potentially for life. Added to that are substantial numbers of failed businesses, bankruptcies, lost fortunes, nervous breakdowns, contracted health maladies, suicides, and premature deaths by various related causes, and the like, just to name some of the consequences experienced by victims. Indeed, the details of the havoc and decimation wreaked upon victims' lives is far too extensive and, frankly, morose to possibly be able to relate here, but suffice it to say it is sweeping, mind-boggling, and, sadly, in some cases, barring the miraculous, irreversible.

The two greatest problems with deception is that the deceived are deceived about being deceived, and their ego and pride make it difficult for them to accept the fact they are in deception. In the case of many of those who do finally accept the fact they have been duped, for years afterward they reel in varied degrees of anger, embarrassment, resentment, disillusionment, and distrust.

No one wants to be a "sucker." Indeed, the sad and unfortunate experience of this ministry in attempting to rescue victims of authoritarian abuse and exploitation is that most simply don't want to hear about anything suggesting they may be deceived, or that their "beloved" church and its leaders to which they have become so dependent could possibly be involved in any kind of deception or error. Even when confronted with proof positive these unscriptural and cult-like teachings and practices are an integral, albeit covert, part of their own church's operations, many indoctrinated adherents react with angry and vehement denial, staunchly refusing to accept even the remotest possibility such a thing could be so.

Moreover, astoundingly, instead of desiring liberation, such "deniers" opt to remain captive in what has become to them the familiar and "friendly confines" of the institution of which they are a member. This sad scenario is strikingly similar to that of many "career criminals" who prefer and choose institutional incarceration over the liberties and latitudes of a normal life of freedom. The constant and abiding prayer of all believers should be that God may grant the captives of all these groups the *"repentance leading to the knowledge of the truth, and they may come to their senses and escape from the snare of the devil, having been held captive by him to do his will"* (2 Tim. 2:26).

Fortunately, though, there are those who, despite their considerable chagrin and pain, *do* want to be liberated from the witchcraft of domination and control, regardless of the cost. Somewhere in the psyche of most sound thinking humans is an intense desire to be free, along with an utter disdain for any form or degree of illegitimate predomination and exploitation.

For those people, there are signs of hyper-authoritarianism that are readily detectable when you know what they are. That is to say, there are a number of common psychological control mechanisms employed within groups in which hyper-authoritarian doctrines and practices are espoused and implemented. Unfortunately, they aren't always simple, overt, and obvious, but are often sophisticated, covert, and hidden. They are, however, identifiable by those who are informed about them and know what to look for.

The purpose of this booklet is to delineate what the common control mechanisms are and how to recognize them. The one thing this booklet cannot supply, though, is the objectivity required to analyze the church or group of which one is a part to determine if these mechanisms are being employed there.

As I close this chapter, I want to state categorically, as I did repeatedly in many ways throughout the original volume from which this booklet was adapted, that I myself am a bona fide Charismatic believer and minister, having never been anything other than that since salvation, and am wholly persuaded of the validity of the Charismatic Movement and its Divine orchestration.

By no means am I engaging in any form or degree of Charismatic-bashing in this booklet. Nor am I denigrating in any form or fashion the Charismatic experience or Biblical teachings restored during the Charismatic Movement.

Rather, I am proffering what I am fully convinced is valid and very much needed God-inspired reproof and correction of patently unscriptural doctrines and practices which unfortunately are being practiced within much of the Charismatic and Neo-Pentecostal Church. That does not mean I am anti-Charismatic or anti-Pentecostal, as some spiritually immature Charismatics are want to allege at the mere hint of criticism of anything relevant to the Charismatic realm or experience. I am neither anti-Charismatic nor anti-Pentecostal, but rather pro both.

My analysis, conclusions, and commentary here or in any of my writings and speaking is not sheer criticism for the purpose of *pillorying* the Charismatic/Pentecostal church, but rather reproof for its *perfection*.

I am also quite aware these doctrines and practices are being espoused and employed in other segments and streams of the Church of Jesus as well. However, it is of the Neo-Pentecostal branch of the Church I am a part, and as such, have a particular "right," yea, even duty, to confront that branch with needed reproof.

It is my deepest desire and heartfelt prayer that all those who name themselves among the Brotherhood of Christ will give heed to the reproof and admonitions presented in this book, and take the actions necessary to liberate the Children of God from the oppressive captivation of men, for they are called to be **SONS** of *God*, not **SLAVE** of *men* (1 Cor. 7:23).

Remember the call of Christ Himself, "If therefore the Son shall make you **FREE**, you shall be **FREE** indeed!" (Jn. 8:36); as well as Paul's echo of Christ's call:

*"It was for **FREEDOM** that Christ set us **FREE**; therefore keep standing firm and do not be subject again to a yoke of slavery" (Gal. 5:1).*

Chapter Two
Religious Enslavement: Sorcery

At the very core of hyper-authoritarian doctrines and practices is religious enslavement. Moreover, let us be clear that religious enslavement is **witchcraft** (aka, sorcery)! Thus, it follows then that hyper-authoritarian doctrines and practices are, at bottom, **witchcraft**! And, that assessment is not at all an extrapolation, but is based on the intrinsic nature of the teachings.

Moreover, it is hardly necessary to point out that witchcraft is something of the devil's domain and not God's. It is this reality that makes these teachings and the practices they promote so decidedly aberrant as well as repugnant to those who are cognizant of it.

Though it be so that these doctrines and practices amount to witchcraft, the problem is, they have already been infused into and become an integral part of the doctrinal and structural system of a large segment of the Charismatic/Pentecostal Body of Christ. Thus the majority of Charismatic/Pentecostal believers, who have been deluded into accepting the validity of them, would have extreme difficulty in understanding and accepting that they are scripturally-invalid and amount to witchcraft, despite the absolute veracity of both of those assessments. Indeed, the very fact that it has been in otherwise legitimate and normative Pentecostal and Neo-Pentecostal (Charismatic, "Word of Faith Movement," and "Third Wave," et al.) churches that these cultic doctrines and practices have been taught and instituted has itself augmented their obscurity and continuance.

Of course, not all Pentecostal or Neo-Pentecostal churches employ these teachings and tactics. Yet, a substantial percentage of especially Neo-Pentecostal churches do, in some form and degree, a percentage much higher than what the average believer would surmise.

In all fairness, I must say there no doubt are some leaders who have accepted and instituted these doctrines and practices in their churches in sincere naivety and ignorance without totally comprehending their full import and impact. Many of those cases are the result of those leaders having blithely "cloned" their ministry structure after someone else's with whom they were associated, affiliated, or simply impressed.

Nevertheless, a significant portion of the leaders who have instituted these errant doctrines and practices have done so with deliberation, knowing fully and precisely what they were doing, having perceived in them a convenient, well-camouflaged, highly effective, and widely-accepted mechanism affording both license and means to predominate and prevail over a group of congregants, in order to enlist and mobilize them as the implementers of their personal kingdom-building. Once wiled, thoroughly indoctrinated, subdued and subjugated, these indentured congregants then become the willful implementers, agents, collaborators, and operatives for the designs of these errant, self-aggrandizing, and self-exalting ecclesiastical autocrats.

The True Nature of Sorcery

Asserting, as I have, that these authoritarian doctrines and practices amount to witchcraft requires that we understand the true nature of witchcraft and sorcery.

"Witchcraft" and "sorcery" are synonymous terms. Some Bible translations use one term, some the other, but both refer to the same thing. The root Greek word for "sorcery" is "pharmakeia," which literally means *to administer drugs*. From this Greek word are derived various English words having to do with medicinal drugs, or narcotics, such as "pharmaceuticals" and "pharmacy."

However, there is a common misconception concerning the nature of witchcraft and sorcery resulting primarily from the etymology of this Greek word translated "sorcery" or "witchcraft" in the New Testament. This word "pharmakeia" was originally coined to allude to the use of narcotics as "mind-altering" and "trance-inducing" intoxicants in pagan religious ceremonies and ministrations throughout the ancient history of paganism.

Notwithstanding, while the original meaning of the word had to do with administering drugs to aid in the casting of spells and inducing trances in pagan occult worship, in the passage of time, it came to have a broader connotation than just that in the Greek language. It came to be what is known as a "metonymn," a figure of speech or kind of colloquialism evoking an idea related to but greater than the literal meaning of the word's components. For example, in the colloquial phrase "under one *roof*," it is not really a literal roof only that is being alluded to, but rather the word "roof" is a metonymn referring to an entire building consisting of walls and a roof. Similarly, both the Greek word "pharmakeia" as well as its English equivalent "sorcery" connote something more than the parochial matter of the use of narcotics in the occult. Rather, it is kind of a "catch-all" phrase evoking the larger concept of *interpersonal predomination and self-imposition* as achieved by various means and methods.

Hence, the Biblical, and thus true spiritual, connotation of sorcery or witchcraft, it is imperative to understand, transcends the use of drugs as an intoxicant or trance-inducer in pagan and occult witchcraft. Biblical sorcery and witchcraft centers more on the specter of people manipulating, dominating, controlling, and captivating other people, whether by supernatural (i.e., demonic) or simply natural (human) means.

To put it another way, while the original meaning of "sorcery" or "witchcraft" had to do with the casting of "spells" or the inducement of "trances" in paganism and the occult, the Biblical usage of these words includes psychological means and methods of usurpation and imposition over others as well. For the truth of the matter is that the "drug" that is used to "cast a spell" over someone is not always a narcotic; there are also a host of psychological means and methods that, especially with the assistance of demons, are just as trance-inducing, compelling, and effective. A "spell" is not just a state of intoxication induced by a narcotic. Rather, a "spell" is any induced condition in which a person's natural and normal self-control over his own thinking and actions is usurped, counteracted, controlled, or simply influenced, by some unnatural, non-indigenous, exterior force. However, the ultimate force behind spells and trances, regardless of the agent, means, or method by which they are induced, is demons and the devil.

Simply stated, the true Spiritual definition and application of "sorcery" or "witchcraft" is using any form of persuasion, influence, intrigue, or inducement, delusion, predomination, or outright coercion, whether of natural (human; psychological) or spiritual (i.e., evil spirits) origin, to unduly and improperly influence, manipulate, dominate, or control someone else, in order to gain ascendancy or advantage for self-aggrandizement. To put it in even simpler terms, sorcery or witchcraft is endeavoring to get someone else to do what *you* want them to do. It is prevailing upon others in order to get them to yield their will to your will. It is volition (will) captivation. It is self-imposition and usurpation. It is being an interloper. It is dominating and controlling others.

God revealed through the prophet Samuel's rebuke of the disobedient King of Israel, Saul, that witchcraft or sorcery is essentially synonymous with "rebellion," and that "disobedience" (which, in essence, is rebellion) is synonymous with "iniquity" (acts of specific trespass and offense against God) and "idolatry" (the imposition of false gods in God's place): *"For* **rebellion** *is as the sin of* **witchcraft***, and* **stubbornness** *(disobedience) is as* **iniquity** *and* **idolatry***"* (1 Sam. 15:23). What this means, in other words, is that witchcraft IS rebellion, and rebellion IS witchcraft; moreover, disobedience (stubbornness) is defiance, disregard, and displacement of God.

The Means and Methods of Sorcery

Now that is the nature of sorcery and witchcraft. But, let's examine now the various means and methods by which sorcery and witchcraft can be effected. Sorcery can be effected either by natural (human) means or by supernatural (demonic) means.

Supernatural means are those means and media involving explicit inducement and abetment by demons. It entails any and all of the manifold satanically-perpetrated occult methods and modes that exist, which range from sensual or sexual seduction to voodoo, from seemingly innocent child's play with a Ouija board or an 8-Ball to séances and consulting mediums, from casual and supposedly "for-amusement-only" reading of newspaper horoscopes to overt, bona fide Satan worship. All of this kind of sorcery and witchcraft is included in the Biblical attribution of "divination." Satan has thoroughly infiltrated this kind of divinational influences and devices into virtually every segment and element of human society and life.

Though this "interpersonal predomination" is sometimes effected through these supernatural means, and witchcraft and sorcery is generally associated with satanic activities, it is vital to understand, however, that to engage in sorcery and witchcraft does not **require** the involvement of supernatural power from demons. Rather, it can also be effected through merely natural, human means emanating out of the human spirit. The unregenerate *human* spirit, permeated as it is with the carnal, sin nature of Satan, intrinsically, certainly is sufficiently evil-prone and evil-proficient in itself to devise and implement devices of unauthorized control over others on its own without any assistance of *demon*-spirits. In the Creational Order, only the Divine Spirit (Nature) of God transcends the human spirit, and being made in the Image of God, the human spirit has some capacity for creativity, though it is limited specifically to the *natural* realm. "Interpersonal predomination" emanating from the human spirit is the natural, human means of sorcery.

Natural, human means would include a wide variety of interpersonal machinations and mechanisms operated in the psychological realm. At one end of that spectrum is an entire range of such machinations and mechanisms falling under the category of what is generally referred to by such terms as "the power of persuasion," which is commonly considered a benign, relatively harmless, fair, and appropriate "art form." Somewhere in the middle of the spectrum is a realm of a kind of Machiavellian "intrigue," it could be called, permeating virtually every segment of life and society from politics to the ministry, wherein the means, no matter how immoral, improper, or unethical, is considered to be justified by the end. At the opposite end of the spectrum, is the more intrinsically sinister and guileful realm of overt predomination by means of a host of psychological mechanisms the object of which is mind-control.

Now, of course, not all "persuasion" is intrinsically evil. There is the benign type of "persuasion" in which one person presents information to another in an attempt to convince that person of the validity of his own perspectives or convictions. However, what makes that kind of inducement benign is that there is no coercion or usurpation of the other person's will involved. The first person is merely presenting to the other person his personal perspective along with supposed corroborative information for the second person's consideration. In the case of illegitimate interpersonal predomination, however, some sort of influence is being covertly injected in order to short-circuit the normal consideration process and to usurp the victim's natural volition (will) for the purpose of subjugation and captivation.

As an aside, within the foregoing also is manifest

the somewhat subtle difference between legitimate *preaching* and *teaching* versus unauthorized *indoctrination* aimed at psychological domination. Ministers have a responsibility to preach the Truth and teach people how to apply the Truth in practical living, but we must never be guilty of in any way alluring or coercing our listeners into ostensible obedience. God desires that we be *obedient* to Him not out of coercion but out of *willingness* (Is. 1:19). Like any human parent, God wants willing obedience from His children. Willing obedience is what brings God pleasure. Coerced obedience really is not *obedience* at all but *compulsion*. The approach of ministers toward their listeners should be the same as God's toward us—we can enjoin, exhort, and evangelize, that is, *call* people to God, but we must never *coerce* or *compel*.

In essence, what this speaks of, is what, indeed, is the very heart of sorcery: the matter of *volition*. The matter of Volitional Authority, or "personal authority," is addressed in some detail in Chapter Four of the book from which this booklet is adapted, *Charismatic Captivation*. It may be helpful to review the commentary on that subject, in that it is related to the topic of this chapter. As indicated there, Volitional Authority is the third highest level of authority God has established in His Creational Order. Only two other types of authority supersede it: God's own sovereignty, and the veracious authority of God's Word.

This personal authority entails the human will, or "free moral agency," as theologians refer to it, with which God has endowed every human being. Essentially, it is the inherent right to personal sovereignty or autocracy, that is, the right to self-government and free-choice. This right, as I stated in Chapter Four, is absolutely inviolable within the restraints of lawfulness. This means that no one but no one has been consigned the right by God to violate or in any way encroach upon the right to self-government vested in each human, as long as that person engages in righteous and lawful conduct, and refrains from engaging in any iniquitous conduct or acts of lawlessness against any other person.

Illustrating the sanctity and absolute inviolability of the human free-will is the fact that, though He certainly is sovereign over all, God Himself will never usurp or in any way forcibly infringe upon the free will of any human being, even when our actions and their consequences are not in our own best interest. Now when we have willingly subjected ourselves unto His Lordship and Fatherhood, as a part of His great Fatherly love for us, He will indeed chasten and discipline us (Heb. 12:5-11). Nevertheless, though He invites *"whosoever will"* affirmatively respond to be adopted into the Heavenly Family, and though He loves us ever so immensely, and deeply desires that all be saved, He will not force Himself, His Sovereignty, nor His Fatherhood, upon any individual, to the point that He will allow us to choose the abyss and agonies of hell over the bliss and blessings of Heaven.

Thus, since the Creator has Himself chosen to grant to every human-being such enormous and unrestrained free agency, in imitating God, as we are enjoined to do by the Word of God (Eph. 5:1, et al.), we the created certainly then are compelled to deal with our fellows in like manner, neither coercing nor in any way imposing our own will upon anyone else. Indeed, to impose our will upon anyone else is the antithesis of the holy and beneficent Divine Nature, and in fact is the very essence of sorcery, which is the essence of the thoroughly unholy, rebellious, and self-seeking nature of Satan.

The Origin of Sorcery

Of course, Satan is the ultimate though unseen source behind every kind and genre of sorcery and witchcraft, and there is an innumerable company of his diabolical cohorts, evil spirits, whose sole function is to perpetrate and propagate witchcraft all throughout the world and among all human beings. However, Satan and his imps can only intervene and invoke their devices in human affairs where and when they are given opportunity, license, and agency by cooperative human-beings. Since God has given authority on the Earth unto the sons of men (Ps. 115:16), Satan is powerless to implement his devices except through human cooperatives.

Sorcery originated with Satan. It is a part of his nature — the spirit of disobedience, *"the spirit that is now working in the sons of disobedience"* (Eph. 2:2). Through the Prophet Isaiah, God revealed by the Spirit what took place when Lucifer fell into apostasy and perdition. His account delineates the precise rebellious ruminations of Lucifer that precipitated his abrupt descent into unrighteousness and spiritual ruin. Clearly, the source of his rebellion is *self-will*, evidenced by the fact that he says to himself five times *"I WILL"*:

> *"But you said in your heart, 'I WILL ascend to heaven; I WILL raise my throne above the stars of God, and I WILL sit on the mount of assembly in the recesses of the north. 'I WILL ascend above the heights of the clouds; I WILL make myself like the Most High.' (Is. 14:13,14)*

This passage makes it clear that rebellion against God (sin) is predicated on self-will or self-imposition.

In essence, rebellion is self-imposition, following after your own will instead of God's. Consequently, it is not hard to understand the meaning of the Spirit's statement: *"Rebellion is as the sin of witchcraft."* In fact, in a broad sense, witchcraft is following after the rebellious nature of Satan, *"the spirit...of disobedience."*

Furthermore, when you put all this together, it becomes clear that Satan's nature is the **Antichrist Spirit**, because it is opposed and antithetical to the Lordship of Christ, and that therefore sorcery and witchcraft is operating in the AntiChrist Spirit. And, indeed that is precisely what sorcery or witchcraft is, endeavoring to be someone's "lord," "master," and "savior" in place of Jesus Christ. That is also why I say, sorcery is self-imposition and usurpation. It is also self-deification, that is, posing and interposing as God, which was precisely what made Lucifer fall into perdition and disenfranchisement from God. Ever since that day when unrighteousness was found in the heart of Lucifer, he has been totally consumed with trying to take Jesus' place as *lord*. He is the ultimate usurper and interloper. He is literally **dying to be god.**

Sorcery Within

If all this concerning sorcery being rooted in the nature of Satan is so, and it is, we must take it a step further. As I mentioned before, no matter how unpalatable to the average believer, the truth is that the nature of the devil, *the spirit of disobedience,* with all its attributes of rebellion and evil, is the carnal nature which pervades the soul of every human being every born. Which means that within us all is the propensity to rebellion, including operating in sorcery and witchcraft. This Truth is corroborated by the Holy Spirit's Words conveyed through the Apostle Paul in his letter to the Galatians, wherein he included *"sorcery"* or *"witchcraft"* (depending on which Bible translation you read) among the attributes of the carnal nature:

> *Now the deeds of the flesh (carnal nature) are evident, which are: immorality, impurity, sensuality, idolatry, **sorcery**, enmities, strife, jealousy, outbursts of anger, disputes, dissensions, factions, envying, drunkenness, carousing, and things like these, of which I forewarn you just as I have forewarned you that those who practice such things shall not inherit the kingdom of God.* (Gal. 5:19-21)

Thus, sorcery, from the spiritual perspective, is not merely an assortment of occult ritual and practices. Rather, sorcery is an attribute of the carnal nature common to us all. To put it another way, sorcery is a natural tendency lurking within the unredeemed soul of every human being which we all are quite capable of operating on our own without any assistance from evil spirits.

Within every one of us mere mortals is the raw desire to in some way and degree predominate and impose our will upon others for our own self-aggrandizing and self-exalting purposes. This propensity is just as much a part of the inherent carnal nature (the source of our temptation to sin) as immorality, enmity, strife, jealousy, anger, or a plethora of other, just as damning, iniquitous attitudes and actions, with which we all, saved or unsaved, are constantly tempted. (In the case of many people, the urge to control others is stronger than their urge to control themselves, as demonstrated by their undisciplined behavior.) The *proclivity*, or in some people, *passion*, to control others is a basic urge of "the roaring lion within" that must be resisted and mastered in the same way as any other evil temptation, else it will surely master and eventually utterly destroy *you*.

Predomination and Control: A Common Element of Religion

Predomination and control has always been a common element of religion. The reason for that is simple. Satan is the ultimate usurper and the real AntiChrist. He is absolutely consumed with the notion of supplanting Jesus as Lord, and establishing himself as lord. He is a million times more crazed by this dastardly fantasy of supreme grandeur than any maniacal tyrant in human history. Religion is the device he uses to deceive people into believing they are right with God, so that he can be lord by default. In actuality, the true though unseen object of religion's homage is demons and the devil. When you pull back the curtain of religion, a la *The Wizard of Oz*, who do you find the wizard has been all along? None other than — **the devil himself!**

Satan is the author of all religion, and *religion* is the counterfeit of *rightstanding* and *relationship* with God. Religion is man's attempts to merit rightstanding with God. Religion, however, does not make you *right* with God, it *separates* you from God. Rightstanding with God cannot be gained on the basis of merit, for every human being who has ever lived, apart from Jesus of Nazareth, has sinned and fallen short of the glory of God. Thus, we need a Savior, and Jesus is the only Savior recognized and sanctioned by God. Everyone who trusts solely in Him to attain rightstanding with God, receives it, on the basis of grace, i.e., undeserved and unmerited favor.

Religion is *self*-justification, in essence. However,

true rightstanding with God is based on *"Jesus-justification,"* that is, justification on the basis of faith in Jesus as the only Savior and the only Way to God.

This is the reason that every religion in the world (what frequently is referred to as "false religion," which is really redundant, because *all* religion intrinsically is false) is fraught with predomination and control. Even Judaism became a debauched religious system wherein the sovereignty of Jehovah was subverted by priests coveting power, prestige, prominence, and preeminence. So also, the functional Headship of Christ was supplanted in early Christianity by the Nicolaitan priesthood, likewise motivated, and their legacy of hierarchical predomination and usurpation is yet an integral part of the fabric of organized Christianity today.

Predomination in the Church

Thus, it comes as no surprise, at least to those who understand the Church is not yet the perfected, blameless, and spotless, Bride it will be at the return of Christ, that the organizational Church, including the supposedly spiritually advanced Pentecostal/Neo-Pentecostal branch, is also tainted by Satanically inspired predomination perpetrated through certain elements of its leadership. Nevertheless, that makes it no less despicable, nor does it diminish in the slightest the Biblical duty of every believer, layman or leader, to proactively and overtly oppose it wherever he or she finds it occurring: *"And do not participate in the unfruitful deeds of darkness, but instead even **expose** them"* (Eph. 5:11).

Having established that all such domination and control is witchcraft or sorcery, as well as examined the nature, origins, means and methods of sorcery, and its inherency in the carnal nature and religion, let us look now at the specific control mechanisms that are commonly employed in hyper-authoritarian groups.

Chapter Three
The Signs of Authoritarian Abuse & Common Control Mechanisms

There are a number of common psychological control mechanisms or methods employed in church-groups in which hyper-authoritarian doctrines are espoused and the attendant practices are implemented. There are also a number of readily identifiable signs indicating that a group is laboring under the heavy hand and oppression of authoritarian abuse. We will examine in this chapter both the control mechanisms and the signs of authoritarian abuse, but before we get to them, I want to briefly discuss the reasons behind the efficacy of these conditions and practices.

Overall, their existence and efficacy has a great deal to do not only with the intrinsic nature of the doctrines and practices themselves, and the seductive powers of the leaders of these groups over their adherents, but also the nature of the spiritual and psychological problems and needs of the individuals who become their unwitting victims. Generally speaking, people seek out and begin attending a church because they have spiritual needs they hope to have met, as well as problems for which they are seeking solutions in the teachings, ministry, activities, and interactivity of the church to which they become affiliated. As unfortunate and unconscionable as it is, it is these very personal needs and problems that these cult-like groups prey upon and exploit with their intricately designed mechanisms and machinations of psychological predomination.

The ensnarement of these psychological captives is analogous to that of the helpless prey snared in the almost invisible silken strands of the spider's web. Immediately upon coming into contact with the sticky strands of the meticulously woven and intricately designed web, the unaware prey becomes a powerless prisoner possessing little chance of escape. In fact, the more the ensnared prey struggles to escape, the more the web's bands collapse upon him, further securing him until the spider can reach the now disoriented and exhausted victim and inject him with the paralyzing venom that will finalize his fate.

A study of the numerous books on cults and false religions that have now been published readily reveal that the techniques and mechanisms of psychological manipulation, domination, and control employed in these groups are strikingly similar, and in some cases identical, to those employed by certified cults. Indeed, to be frank about it, many of these groups and churches employ these techniques and mechanisms so overtly that they are themselves at the very minimum quasi-cults, and in some cases, bona fide cults, despite the dismay and vehement denials their leaders and followers alike express when confronted with the similarity of the doctrines and practices employed in their own church to those commonly employed within these certified cults.

The thing that utterly astounds me in the matter, is that even when you provide proof-positive to adherents that these unbiblical and cult-like teachings and practices are an integral, albeit covert, part of the fabric and foundation of their own church, ministry, or network, many react with angry and vehement denial, staunchly refusing to accept even the remotest possibility that such a thing could be so of their "beloved" church or ministry, and opt, rather, to remain a captive in what has become to them the familiar and "friendly confines" of the institution of which they are a member. This sad scenario bears striking similarity to the admitted mindset of many "career criminals" who have become such complete psychopathic derelicts that they prefer and choose institutional incarceration over the liberties and latitudes of a normal life of freedom.

Nevertheless, my constant and abiding prayer, and indeed the objective of all the protracted and tedious labor that has gone into the production of this volume, is that God may grant some of the captives of these groups the *"repentance leading to the knowledge of the truth, and they may come to their senses and escape from the snare of the devil, having been held captive by him to do his will"* (2 Tim. 2:26).

It is toward the accomplishment of that goal that I delineate in this chapter some of the more salient signs and symptoms of authoritarian abuse as well as the most common techniques and mechanisms of manipulation, domination, and control employed within these groups. To describe them so explicitly and precisely as I do will seem to some judgmental and censorial, especially to those to whom they will be as a mirror reflecting their own attitudes and conduct, as well as those who are or have been adherents of organizations in which these doctrines and practices were or are espoused and employed. But, criticizing and condemning the perpetrators and participants is not the purpose of presenting them, nor is that my place or even desire. Rather, the purpose of clearly identifying these signs of authoritarian abuse and religious enslavement as well as the attendant common control mechanisms simply is to enable readers to recognize them so that they can avoid entities wherein they are manifested. My role here is to spotlight these patently erroneous and spiritually harmful doctrines and deeds, and it's God's role to spotlight the motives and intents of the heart of practitioners in order to lead them to repentance.

The Signs and Symptoms of Authoritarian Abuse

The following are some of the general signs and symptoms, or common characteristics, of hyper-authoritarian groups, churches, networks, and ministries. Bear in mind that the list is by no means exhaustive, and that these are general, rather than, exact descriptions.

1. Apotheosis or de facto deification of the leadership — exalting them to God-like status in and over the group, often to the extent that the leaders become a "mediator" between the people and God;
2. MLM-like multi-level authority/government hierarchy (chain-of-command);
3. Absolute authority of the leadership to the extent that the effect is a suspension of independent thought and Berean-like examination of Scripture to verify the correctness of the teaching of the leadership;
4. No real accountability of the leadership to the corporate body, resulting in a repressive monarchical (autocratic, dictatorship) or oligarchic form of government;
5. Hand-picked sub-leaders, based on their demonstration of submissiveness to the ultimate

leader rather than on the basis of their leadership skills, spirituality, and anointing and appointment by God;
6. Pervasive abuse and misuse of authority in personal dealings with members to coerce submission;
7. Paranoia, inordinate egotism or narcissism, and insecurity by the leaders;
8. Abuse, misuse, and inordinate incidence of "church discipline," particularly matters not expressly mentioned in the Bible as church discipline issues;
9. Personal materialism, covetousness, and self-aggrandizement by the leaders, particularly when the personal lifestyle of the leader(s) is well-beyond the median lifestyle of the membership and that lifestyle is underwritten primarily from donations received from the membership;
10. Members and/or sub-leaders must make a "spiritual covenant," sometimes a signed covenant agreement, pledging their total and everlasting commitment and financial support to the leadership and church/ministry;
11. Partitioning of the congregation into smaller groups that are led by internally "raised up" and appointed lay-leaders who have not been anointed or appointed by God for leadership within the church, i.e., Fivefold Ministers;
12. Financial exploitation and enslavement of the members, often by requiring or coercing them to donate well-beyond their means and Biblical principles;
13. Inordinate attention to maintaining the public "image" of the ministry and lambasting of all "critics";

14. Doctrinal demeanment and devaluation — the Biblical requisite of espousing and teaching "sound doctrine" in accordance with Scripture is demeaned and devalued in order to justify or suspend evaluation of unorthodox or unproven doctrines and private interpretations of Scripture taught by the leadership;
15. Theological incompetency by the leadership, especially with respect to the accepted rules of hermeneutics and Biblical exegesis employed in the formulation of doctrine, giving license to twisting and adulteration of Scripture in order to provide proof-texts for unorthodox and self-invented doctrines;
16. Spiritualism, mysticism, and unproven or anti-biblical doctrines;
17. Abuse and misuse of prophetic giftings as a means to dominate and intimidate;
18. Devaluation, disallowance, disregard, and displacement of the true Fivefold Ministry within the church;
19. De facto legalism, or works mentality, and its resulting loss of the "joy of salvation," though "freedom" is forever preached from the pulpit and the church is constantly touted as being a "safe church" by the leadership;
20. Esotericism—hidden agendas and requirements revealed to members only as they successfully advance through various stages of "spiritual enlightenment," which in fact is really unorthodox, unproven indigenous doctrines;
21. Isolationism—corporate and individual, especially with respect to exposure to outside ministry sources;
22. Performance-based approval and promotion system of members predicated on "proven"

"loyalty" (i.e., submission) to the leadership;
23. Devaluation, suppression, and non-recognition of members' bona fide God-given talents, abilities, gifts, callings, and anointing, as a means of subjugation;
24. Requiring members to perform menial tasks, such as cleaning toilets, setting up chairs, and acting as the leader's personal valet or slave, as a supposed means to humble them and teach them to "obey their leaders" or to evaluate their willingness to "submit to authority;"
25. Constant indoctrination with a "group" or "family" mentality that impels members to exalt the corporate "life" and goals of the church-group over their personal goals, callings, objectives, and relationships;
26. Members are psychologically traumatized and indoctrinated with numerous improper fears and phobias aimed at keeping them reeling in diffidence and an over-dependence or co-dependence on their leaders and the corporate group;
27. Corporately, there eventually develops an inordinately high incidence of financial, marital, moral, psychological, mental, emotional, and medical problems, including sudden deaths and contraction of "incurable" and "unknown" diseases;
28. Lack of true personal spiritual growth and development, especially in terms of genuine faith and experiencing the abounding grace, forgiveness, goodness, blessings, kindness, and agape-love of God;
29. Members are required to obtain the approval or "witness" of their leader(s) for decisions regarding personal matters;

30. Frequent preaching from the pulpit regarding not getting out from under the "spiritual covering" of the leadership by leaving the church/group or disobeying the leaderships' dictates and demands of you;
31. Members departing without the prior permission and blessing of the leadership leave the group under a cloud of manufactured suspicion, shame, and slander;
32. Horror stories frequently told by leaders about individuals or families who left the group without the prior permission and blessing of the leadership, and the terrible consequences and curses they suffered as a result;
33. Departing and ostracized members often suffer from various psychological problems and display the classic symptoms associated with Post-Traumatic Stress Disorder (PTSD).

If after reading this list and recognizing doctrines and practices your church or ministry is engaging in, and you have great difficulty admitting it, even to yourself, then you are definitely brainwashed and under the spell of "deceitful spirits and doctrines of demons," and these demonic lies are "seared in your own conscience as with a branding iron" (1 Tim. 4:1,2). And, that means you need **deliverance** to be set free from Satan's bondage and deception. It also means you are deceived about who you are serving. You are not serving the true Jesus, who is the One who died to set the captives free, but rather you are serving false gods — **idols** — which is **idolatry**, which means you are an "idolater," and idolaters do not inherit eternal life or have an inheritance in the Kingdom of Christ and God (Gal. 5:20,21; Eph. 5:5)! The only way for you to escape HELL and eternal punishment, and enter into Heaven and the Kingdom, is to

repent! Then **run** from your captors and **rush** into the arms of the True Jesus, who died to set the captives **FREE!** "**He whom the Son sets FREE is FREE INDEED!**"

The Common Control Mechanisms

We turn our attention now to the common control mechanisms employed within these hyper-authoritarian groups. Remember as you study them that, as previously mentioned, the premise of "absolute submission," which is the bedrock of such authoritarian doctrines, coupled with the enslaving organizational and authority structure are the primary components that make these techniques and mechanisms effectual and effective.

Just one other comment before we get to them. As you will readily notice, the primary force behind these subjugation techniques and mechanisms of manipulation and their common denominator is **fear.** This in itself is Satan's unmistakable signature and seal that distinguishes all that is demonic from that which is from God, for all of Satan's works are predicated upon and produce *fear,* whereas all that God does is founded in and produces *faith.*

1. Apotheosis of the Leadership.

Apotheosis means to exalt something or someone to divine rank or stature, or in other words to *deify.* This is precisely what takes place in bona fide cults, as well as in groups where excessive authoritarianism is practiced—*de facto* deification of the leadership. In these groups, the leadership are exalted to a status tantamount to being equal with God within the structure and internal operations of that group.

For all intents and purposes the chief leader of that group IS "God," in that his authority is absolute.

What he says goes. The authority of the leader and his delegates is absolute and unchallengeable, and its scope gradually expands to the point of eventually becoming all-encompassing, affecting every segment of their followers' lives. The truth, however, as indicated throughout this volume, is that God and the Word of God is the only true and valid authority over any adult, law-abiding human—believer or unbeliever. Moreover, the "authority" of the intermediaries (ministers) God works through is limited to the spiritual realm and to the very parochial bounds of the government or administration of the specific spiritual "house" (i.e., local church or ministry) over which they preside.

In groups where this totally fallacious concept of leadership apotheosis has been successfully instituted, it casts a very long and imposing shadow of total domination and subjugation over the entire congregation. The power of this religious predomination lays in the purported premise that to disobey the dictates and desires of the leadership is to disobey and defy God Himself, in that those leaders are the literal representations of Christ Himself, much in the same way as the Pope is regarded in Catholicism.

Indeed, as if on cue, just a few days prior to the editing of these words in the original version, one of the "tabloid news" television programs did a story on a scandal taking place in a prominent Charismatic church in Atlanta led by a very well-known "Bishop" and founder of the ICCC International College of Bishops, in which several female former administrative-staffers charged several of the church's top leaders with various forms of sexual misconduct perpetrated under the color of ministerial authority. In attempting to explain how it was that these adult, responsible, presumably intelligent, sincere Christians could have been seduced by the alleged adulterous advances of these clerical-collared clergymen, one of the alleged victims responded with tears of apparent remorse and shame flowing down her flushed face: "These men were like God to us. We were taught that whatever they said was right, and **to disobey them was to disobey God.**" This situation is a glaring example of the kind of abuse of authority that can result from improper and undue exaltation of spiritual leaders.

2. Fear and Intimidation Projection

In these hyper-authoritarian groups wherein there is a culture of domination and control, members are psychologically traumatized and indoctrinated with numerous fears and phobias aimed at keeping them reeling in diffidence and dependence on their leaders and the corporate group. So intense are these fears and phobias that departing members commonly suffer from various psychological problems and even clinical neuroses, and some even display the classic symptoms associated with Post-Traumatic Stress Disorder (PTSD). Following their departure or separation from the group, in addition to deliverance from demonic incursion, many have a need for some form of psychological counseling. The following are some of the fears the leadership of these groups foster and project upon their adherents as a form of subjugation.

A. Fear of Open Censure and Rebuke.

Various forms and degrees of public reproof, censure, chastisement, remonstration, and even open rebuke of members whom the leadership has deemed to be wayward, errant, and "rebellious," are a common practice in both Discipleship/Shepherding groups and other cults. Members who do not toe the line with complete obedience to every rule, regulation, code, and dictate passed down through the leadership are branded by the leaders with the Scarlet Letter "*R*" for "Rebellious," and are publicly reprimanded—in the smaller cell-group meetings, sometimes from the (bully-)pulpit in the main meetings of the entire assembly.

This ever-looming threat of prospective public humiliation and censure becomes a very effective means of predomination by intimidation to the entire membership. No one dare disobey or even question the dictates of, or speak a critical word against, the leadership of the church, lest the "critic" be subjected to this public dressing down.

Open rebuke should be an extreme *rarity* and last *resort*, and certainly should not become *routine*. Scripture prohibits it except in the most egregious cases of persisting overt hypocrites, factious strife-bearers, and egregiously errant elders.

B. Fear of Disapproval and Rejection.

This is very similar and related to the previous type of fear that is projected, as well as intertwined with all the others. Members live in constant fear of getting on the wrong side of the leadership and receiving their disapproval and hence being rejected by them and/or their fellow members.

The prospect of finding real solutions and resolution for very real spiritual and psychological (i.e, pertaining to the soul) and spiritual needs and infirmities often is a primary motivation of many people as they search for a church-group to become related to in the first place. They come looking for love, acceptance, and remedy of their deepest spiritual and psychological needs. But it is often these very needs and infirmities that make such people vulnerable to the exploitation and predomination perpetrated by these types of authoritarian groups. And, no one perhaps is more vulnerable to such exploitation and predomination than the person who suffers from a spirit of rejection and its accompanying *fear* of rejection and fear of disapproval. A sense of rejection is a "bottomless well" that is never filled regardless of how much love is poured into it. My personal view is that exploiting people who have such a real need for real ministry is as vile and reprehensible as it gets, and I know from many years of personal experience in dealing with this problem that multitudes of others share that view.

Groups employing hyper-authoritarian doctrines often practice some form and degree of "shunning," a highly effective technique of punitive manipulation through group-ostracism that for ages has been a common practice within false religious sects and cults. Shunning is when a group scorns and disassociates from a member as a kind of chastisement and disapproval for some aspect of conduct considered improper by the group. It can come in the form of disdain, scorn, snubbing, avoidance, aloofness, outright exclusion, rebuffing, "looking off on," "giving the cold shoulder," distancing, slighting, and ignoring. Whatever the form it takes, everyone knows instinctively when he is being shunned. To the insecure and diffident, the effects of such overt disdain and disapprobation can be overwhelming and devastating. It is certainly telling that many pseudo-Christian sects such as the Quakers regard the practice as a legitimate rite of chastisement of wayward members.

In hyper-authoritarian groups, fellow members shun members whose conduct has merited them the attribution of "rebellious" as a mechanism of open chastisement and intimidation, with the aim of *sham-*

ing the offender into getting back into line. In order to get back into the good graces of the group, those who subject themselves to and succumb to this vile form of sorcery, typically, must endure the public humiliation of confessing their errancy before the entire assembly and begging forgiveness of the leaders and group. While to the casual observer this mechanism of manipulation may seem not so egregious, to members of these religious mini-societies who are constantly striving for acceptance and fellowship, the effects of exclusion and ostracism by fellows can be psychologically traumatizing and spiritually devastating, making it a potent weapon of predomination in the hands of the malevolently motivated.

C. Fear of Denunciation and Disgrace Upon Departure.

When anyone leaves one of these groups of their own volition for whatever reason without the approval and consent of the leadership (which usually is granted only in the case of employment-related transfer or death), or for a reason that is not acceptable to the leadership, those persons are almost always branded "rebels" by the leadership, and the reason for their departure is declared to be "rebellion."

"Departees" whose departure is predicated on disagreement with the doctrines espoused and practices employed by the group, are invariably labeled as having "a critical spirit," and their criticisms are declared to be invalid and unmerited and emanating from a rebellious and critical spirit. Harmonious and peaceable parting of the ways is virtually non-existent, as the jilted and chagrined leadership invariably feels compelled to disparage the "departees" and to declare them *persona non grata in perpetuity*, forbidding contact with them by any of the remaining membership.

The prospect of such denunciation and discrediting by the leadership can be especially disconcerting to those called to the ministry who find themselves in the position of having to depart the group in obedience to a calling from God. In such cases the viability of both those persons' ministry and their livelihood can be very really affected by the acts of censure, condemnation, denouncement, anathematizing, retribution, recrimination, and black-listing made by the scorned former leadership. Very often those are not merely idle threats, but rather, especially in the case of an itinerant ministry, because of the "political" nature of the ministry, a "black-listed" minister can indeed have many doors of ministry closed to him, regardless of the validity and quality of his ministry, merely on the basis of having been dubbed a "rebel" by some scorned ecclesiastical autocrat or the ubiquitous *"Neo-Pentecostal La Cosa Nostra."*

D. Fear of Excommunication.

In the face of the prospect of such consequences of denunciation as those delineated in the foregoing, the specter of similar humiliation, disparagement, and repudiation resulting from excommunication then also becomes a very real and formidable threat looming over the head of every member. This is especially so after their entire life and that of their family has become intertwined and immersed in their church-community.

However, the ironic truth of the matter is that because of their desperation to keep every member as a part of the fold, rarely do these kinds of groups actually excommunicate anyone. Instead of excommunication, they implement various other of the techniques and mechanisms delineated here to attempt to intimidate any would-be "rebellious" members into compliance and submission.

E. Fear of Judgment.

In addition to all the above factors, members are incessantly indoctrinated with the premise that if they ever leave the church or group without the approval of the leadership, they will incur the wrath of God and be under His judgment, which will result in terrible things happening to them because they are under a curse from God.

Laced into sermons, "orientation" classes, and various person-to-person conversations among the members, are melodramatic horror stories of people who "got out from under the covering" of their leader and church community, and who because of that experienced terrible curses and judgments in their lives. These stories are cited to illustrate that members should never even think of leaving the group, for fear of all the terrible things that will happen to them if they do.

Aside from the fact that this is precisely what members of cults and occult initiates are told, this is a totally false and unfounded claim for several reasons. First of all, as it was painstakingly proven in Chapter Five of *Charismatic Captivation*, the premise of "spiritual covering" as taught in the Discipleship doctrines is a total fallacy and myth. Our covering, or hedge of providential care and protection, does not come in any way shape or form from any human-being, or group of human-beings, but from God alone:

> *HE will cover you with HIS pinions, and under HIS wings you may seek refuge; HIS faithfulness is a SHIELD AND BULWARK [an impenetrable rampart of protection]. I will say TO THE LORD, 'My REFUGE and my FORTRESS, my GOD in*

*whom I trust.' For it is **HE** who delivers you from the snare of the trapper [Satan], and from the deadly pestilence. (Ps. 91:4,2; brackets and emphasis added by author)*

We are to glory and take solace in the fact that we dwell under the *shelter* (protective covering) of the Most High God and that we therefore abide (continuously live) in the *shadow* of the Almighty God (from which devils flee): *"He who dwells in the **shelter** of the Most High will abide in the **shadow** of the Almighty"* (Ps. 91:1). It is **HIS** shelter and shadow, which are of and exist in the spiritual realm, that are the only valid and impervious protection against the attacks of the enemy that are levied in the spiritual realm. No human shelter and shadow, whether of an individual or a group, offers any protection whatsoever against such attacks perpetrated by evil-spirits in the spirit realm.

Second, God does not bring judgment upon a person or a family simply because they leave a particular church or group. There is absolutely no Biblical corroboration of the ridiculous claim that He does; rather, it is a totally unfounded myth. Leaving a particular group or church, for whatever reason, is **not** tantamount to abandoning **the** Church or falling away from God, as these groups allege. No church or group is that sacrosanct. Every true believer has been "baptized" or immersed by the Holy Spirit into the Body of Christ, whether they are a member of a church-organization or not.

The true Church of Jesus Christ is not an inanimate *organization* or even a conglomeration of church-organizations. Rather, the true Church is a living *organism* comprised of true believers. Being a member of and engrossed in the community of some humanly-invented and -run church-organization and assembly in no way certifies, enhances, or has any bearing whatsoever on your eternal fellowship with God, but rather it is having been made a bona fide member of and immersed in *"the general assembly and church of the first-born"* (Heb. 12:23) that certifies and seals your eternal destiny and destination.

Frequent fellowship with some segment of the true Brotherhood is highly recommended and certainly synergistically beneficial, but it will not save us. We fellowship, worship, and receive from the Lord in corporate gatherings because salvation is the common denominator among us. However, absolutely no requisites regarding either the place of worship or the number of the worshipers are delineated anywhere in the Bible. On the contrary, though staunch "organizationalists" consumed with increasing the membership of their organizations hate the veracity and validity of it, remember that Jesus Himself vowed that He would personally attend and be in the midst of any meeting conducted in His Name, even if the number of those gathered together was only *"two or three"* (Mat. 18:20), and He made that vow without any reference to the place where that meeting was held. Jesus explicitly stated that *"true worshipers"* were those who *"worship the Father in Spirit and in Truth* [i.e., in accordance with sound doctrine]*"* (Jn. 4:23). Validity of worship is not determined by the place of worship or the number of the worshipers, but by whether or not it is inspired by the Holy Spirit and in accordance with the Truth of God's Word.

Thirdly, God allows all believers the latitude to make their own choices with regard to the group with which they identify, on the basis of congruity with their particular personalities, spiritual needs, interests, and emphasis, as long as the group they choose is grounded in sound doctrine and practices. Despite the absolute falseness of this notion, the prospect of being subject to circumstantial Divine judgment remains a very effective weapon for making indoctrinated members of these groups paralyzingly fearful of ever leaving the group.

F. Fear of Failure.

A constant undercurrent of the teaching, counseling, and communal conversation within these groups is the cultivation and reinforcement of a fear of failure if members do not obediently and docilely follow every rule and dictate emanating from the leadership as a whole, as well as every personal command of each leader comprising the multiplicity of echelons of leaders over the group.

These groups thrive on condescension and berating of the capabilities and judgment of the members, juxtaposed to that of their "spiritually superior" leaders. Instead of declaring *release*, forgiveness, restoration, and overcoming of past faults, failures, and tendencies, as the Gospel of Good News prescribes, in these groups there is a constant and continual *reminding* of past faults, failures, weaknesses, and tendencies. "Remember now," leaders say to their subjects, "you've always had a problem with...(this or that)." Or, "You know you've always been rebellious...." And so on.

The ultimate purpose of this constant identification with failure is to create within the members a profound sense of dependency on the group and its leaders to make their decisions for them and to tell them what is best for them. Adding to the problem is the fact that there certainly is no shortage of lazy and negligent people, and those who refuse to repent of the fear of failure, who are quite content to have someone else tell them everything to do, rather than have to seek the Lord for themselves as to the specificities of their lives.

G. Fear of Lost or Invalid Salvation.

Typically in these groups—wherein extreme and aberrant authoritarian doctrines requiring "absolute submission" to the leadership are relentlessly hammered into their heads, and a yoke of overbearing, unrealistic, and unscriptural dictates, demands, and expectations is placed upon their necks—members' salvation is under constant challenge and doubt. In time, they begin to question whether or not they were ever really saved in the first place, or whether they have subsequently lost their salvation and rightstanding with God, because of their purported propensity to "rebellion."

Their instinctive and intuitive inclinations to reject the demonic and unnatural enslavement to which they are being subjected, they are told, is nothing but their "rebellion to authority" continuing to rise up within them, which they must conquer, and learn to "just submit." They are incessantly barraged with charges of being a "rebel," and that their "rebellion" against the oppressive domination being perpetrated upon them is evidence of and resulting from their rebellion against *God.*

This extremely disconcerting uncertainty, and in some cases, tormenting fear, concerning the validity and genuineness of their salvation, is used as a very effective means of keeping the ever-diffident members docile and cowering.

3. Guilt Projection.

Related to and used in concert with the aforementioned, guilt projection, essentially, is a method of manipulation or control in which an abstract but nonetheless effectual, ever-present sense of guilt is purposely projected upon subjects by the subjugator.

It is employed on two fronts within these groups. First, on the personal level, wherein members are continually battered and psychologically abused with regard to their sinfulness and rebellious attitudes, for which no real forgiveness and redemption is ever extended or reinforced by the leadership. This causes the members to labor under a perpetual cloud of guilt, unworthiness, rejection, and total exasperation. Consequently, members embark upon a never-ending merry-go-round ride of vain fleshly works, trying and failing over and over again to "measure up" and thereby *merit* the forgiveness and acceptance of God, their group-peers, and their leaders. This is used as a mechanism of manipulation to keep the members forever docile, doting, and drudging, as approval and acceptance are tantalizingly dangled before them, just out of their reach, like the mechanical rabbit at a dog race.

Second, members are constantly told how vital their own participation and financial support is to the overall success of the church and its every "mission." Through very skillful oratorical wheedling, members are cajoled into personal identification with the contrived plans, projects, and programs of the church, all of which are adamantly alleged to be God-inspired and God-sponsored. Members are craftily lured into accepting the hypothesis that since these plans, projects, and programs came directly and purely from God as a Divinely-inspired mission and assignment for the group, and since they are a member of the group, the success of the mission is their *personal* responsibility. If the project or program is not successfully completed, it is the personal fault of each and every member, for which God holds them personally accountable, even though the individual members never personally heard from God regarding the matter, and were never even given the option of testing whether or not this matter truly was from God for themselves, as Scripture requires, or a means by which to express their view.

4. Isolation.

The Great Wall of China and the former Berlin Wall, are classic examples of walls that were built by would-be world emperors not only to keep peoples of other lands along with their opposing ideologies *out*, but to keep their own people *in*, and to thereby insulate them from influences contrary to the particular utopia-promising political ideologies they were promulgating.

The same is true of the invisible but very real walls of religious segregation in the form of denominationalism and other kinds of sectarianism erected throughout the Church Age by ecclesiastical prefects out of intense insecurity and paranoia, in many cases to the point of neurosis, in the hope of keeping their followers from being exposed and attracted to teaching and experiences contradictory to the particular ideologies and dogmas they were promoting.

Classic cults, especially during the indoctrination stage, require virtually complete isolation of the inductee from family and friends in order to insulate them from all contradictory influences. Similarly, hyper-authoritarian groups strongly urge their members to avoid fellowship with anyone who is not a part of their group, including fellow-believers, friends, and especially family. Attending another church, without the prior approval and consent of their leaders (which is almost never granted) is cause for censure and possible "disfellowship," or excommunication. In some groups, even the reading of books, viewing television programs, and listening to radio programs of other ministers is prohibited without the consent of the leadership and unless that other ministry has been "approved" by the leadership of the group (and, of course, very, very few are).

Of course, the common claim of those who preach and require such segregation and isolation is that this is a very noble and beneficial protective measure instituted in the members' best interest in order to protect them from deceiving and damaging influences. However, nowhere does the Word of God teach that either segregation or isolation is a deterrent or preventative against spiritual deception. Rather, Jesus explicitly said that if a person *"abides"* (i.e., hears and obeys, lives) in the Word of God, **THEN** that person would *"know the Truth,"* and **THE TRUTH** would set *that* person—the person who knows the Truth of God's Word—free, which includes setting them free and keeping them free from deception (Jn. 8:31,32). In other words: It is **TRUTH**, that sets free! Truth *never* deceives or enslaves!

Groups that mandate or urge separation and isolation from other segments of the true Body of Christ, as well as those, I might add, that promote communal-living, are dangerous! Sincere and earnest believers would do well to avoid all such groups because this especially is one of the common earmarks of cults.

5. Internalization.

One consistent hallmark of these groups is extremism regarding personal involvement and participation of every member. Getting every person deeply involved in some function, or duty, or role of participation is a virtual obsession with these groups. Programs and departments are created for the primary purpose of keeping every member of every family engrossed in some type of in-house involvement, which they refer to as "ministries," from music to recreation to special study programs to an infinite number of other specialty ministries.

The premise is, of course, that the more *involved* a person is and the more *important* he or she feels, the greater and more intent will be his or her personal *commitment* and *contribution* to the overall operations and machinery of the organization. And, indeed, usually, the plan works precisely as designed, producing the intended results. The primary reason for that is that they exploit three very basic human desires: the need to feel accepted and part of something, the need to feel important and needed, and the need to function and be fruitful, that is, accomplish something meaningful. If not sanctified through the Cross of Christ and fulfilled through the Life of Christ, these desires are nothing more than selfish ambition, which is a primary inroad for Satanic exploitation.

Someone may well say, "But, every church tries to get its members involved, is that always wrong?" The answer is that every believer has a God-given spiritual function both in the church and in the world (Eph. 4:16; Rom. 12:6-8; 1 Pet. 4:10; et al.), but these are real and spiritually effectual functions bearing true spiritual fruit that remains (Jn. 15:16), not silly, superficial, artificial, and spiritually inconsequential, internal ecclesiastical dabbling, producing virtually no true spiritual fruit, but serving only to stroke the participant's already overinflated ego and superfluous sense of self-importance.

6. Economic Exploitation and Enslavement.

It is an incontrovertible fact that the Bible is replete with passages and promises concerning abundant financial blessing coming unto those who are faithful in their tithing and giving, and in the administration of "unrighteous mammon" (money). Indeed, everyone who has perseveringly and faithfully complied with the requisites and conditions of those promises can attest to their validity and absolute trustworthiness.

It is a certainty that God desires to bless His people financially, and He has established the spiritual law of sowing and reaping (Gen. 8:22; Gal. 6:7) or *"giving and receiving"* (Lk. 6:38; Plp. 4:15) as the primary means through which to accomplish that blessing. The long and the short of the ordinance is that when a believer sows financially, He will in due season reap a multiplied financial harvest commensurate with the amount of seed sown. Thus, every believer should be a consistent and persistent sower. So, in no way am I denigrating the very valid truths in the Word of God regarding giving our tithes and offerings with this point about this manipulation mechanism.

However, in both classical cults as well as groups such as those churches we are discussing of the Pentecostal and Neo-Pentecostal community who employ these practices of overt control and domination, there is almost invariably an aberrant ilk of "stewardship" espoused that places excessive demands and requirements upon the members for monetary contributions to the group, and for "accountability" regarding their personal financial matters. Members are incessantly pressed to give more and more beyond their ten percent tithe in special offerings to fund an endless litany of special in-house "ministries and missions," projects, and programs. In addition, cell-group leaders keep a very watchful eye on the personal expenditures of the members of their group, in many cases interposing their own unqualified, non-professional, and unsolicited advice with regard to what should be members' private financial affairs. As mentioned before, it is a documented fact that in some Shepherding groups, the leaders, despite not having any training or expertise in financial matters, are the members' de facto financial advisors, and members are essentially constrained from making important financial transactions without the advice and consent of their leader(s), which advice is usually weighted toward *frugality* with respect to the members' expenditure of their money on their own needs and *liberality* with respect to the needs of the church or ministry.

7. Dependence Indoctrination.

The primary purpose and goal of many, if not all, of the aforementioned techniques and mechanisms of manipulation is to produce in the adherents a psychological dependence on the group and especially the leader. Members are taught to put all their faith, hope, and trust in the groups' leaders, which is idolatry, and actually grants opportunity and permission for invasion by all manner of evil spirits, not the least of which is the spirit of fear. As a result of these techniques and mechanisms, members are terrified by the prospect of punitive action that they have been taught would be emanating ultimately from God Himself if they are not completely submissive to every dictate and whim of their leaders, they are laden with overwhelming burdens of false guilt, isolated from other sources of Truth and fellowship, and their entire life is totally immersed in the internal involvements of that group. The outcome is an ungodly, unscriptural, and even demonic, all-encompassing spiritual and psychological dependency on the group and the leader.

What leaders of such groups purport to be exhorting their members to in this regard, is the quite virtuous, laudable, and desirable qualities of "allegiance," "loyalty," and "commitment" elemental to what they refer to as "covenantal relationships." However, the truth is that, as discussed previously, these "covenantal relationships" are actually "covenants with demons" that are not based in true freedom and the attributes of the Spirit, but in seduction, witchcraft, bondage, and captivation inspired by evil spirits. Moreover, the outcome certainly is not a working of the *Holy* Spirit, for the Bible clearly proclaims that, *"where the Spirit of the Lord is, there is liberty"* (2 Cor. 3:17), not bondage.

Once ensnared in the web of bondage and dependency, the victim of these control mechanisms is mentally, emotionally, and spiritually dependent, not on the Father, Son, and Holy Ghost, but on the human leaders and fellow members of his group for psychological satisfaction and survival in every aspect of life. This is spiritual treachery and apostasy of the highest order.

8. Esotericism.

With these cult-like groups, there is a deliberate and carefully crafted concealment or obfuscation of the group's true nature, agenda, and modus operandi from the general public as well as prospective recruits and new proselytes. The complete truth is known only to the few who are part of an elite and exclusive "inner circle" of compatriots. This is the very definition of "esotericism," which tellingly has been deemed by the highest courts of our land in cases where legal action has been taken against such religious cults and illegal pyramid schemers to constitute criminal fraud.

Full disclosure is not made up front, but comes only incrementally as the initiate advances through the various levels of "orientation" and "enlightenment" that are supposedly required for full comprehension of the teachings and methodologies of the group. Obscuring and skewing of these particulars concerning the group to the general public are ostensibly justified by the assertion that comprehension of the import of the group's teachings and purposes requires the "enlightenment" that comes only to those who have been fully trained (in reality, indoctrinated and brainwashed) by the teachings and dogmas comprising their belief system.

The real crux of the deceitfulness and dastardliness of this incremental disclosure lies in the fact that it is not until the passenger has boarded the ship, and it has set sail and begun traversing the great abyss of irrational indoctrination, that he is informed of the destination and full cost of the voyage, metaphorically speaking. It is perhaps revealing that this incremental disclosure technique is a watermark of classic modern cults, many of whom now, because of widespread discreditation and negative publicity, have resorted to a variety of actions aimed at improving their public image, including organizational name changes, the use of euphemistic terminology, more sophisticated concealment of true intents and purposes, and plain old outright *lying*.

9. "Love Bombing."

I don't know who is credited with the original coining of the term "love bombing," but it is a term often evoked in contemporary descriptions of the psychological techniques employed by classic cults to woo new recruits, and to maintain the bonds of enslavement on existing members. The so-called "love" that is spoken of in these groups is an ushy-gushy, sickly-sweet, surreal, over-done, showy, carnal, humanistic kind of "sloppy-agape," replete with a superabundance of hugging and cheek-kissing.

In a way similar to the classic cults, proselytes are lured into the group by means of an auspicious, blissful, ethereal, soulish, and sensory-appealing "love" that is presented as the ultimate in "freedom." In bona fide cults, this so-called "love" is so "free," that is, without limitations, that it invariably translates eventually into unrestrained and promiscuous immorality, or "free-love," which some cults proclaim to be one of the many "benefits" and "privileges" of their purportedly transcendent brand of "spiritual enlightenment." Sadly, there have been some Christian groups of the ilk of which we have been speaking that in the process of time as they traveled down the path of error and errancy have become deceived by the same seducing evil spirits, eventually engaging in the same scurrilous debauchery as well. More and more of such cases are being publicly exposed to the light, as well they should be (Eph. 5:11; 1 Tim. 5:19,20; et al.), despite the long shadow of reproach it casts upon all of Christendom.

In addition to utilizing this "love bombing" technique on prospective proselytes, in these quasi-cultish groups, the leaders and "indoctrinators" constantly bombard members and initiates with this soulish, sensual love as a kind of sedative to anesthetize them against the effects of the control mechanisms and techniques, and to keep them oblivious to the fact that these devices of domination are being imposed upon them. This false "love" becomes an immensely effective "psychological-pharmaceutical" by which the indoctrinated members are drugged and induced into accepting the harsh and overbearing domination and control techniques as being beneficent and beneficial expressions of this anomalistic "love."

10. Personal Predomination.

This common control mechanism essentially involves the usurpation of the personal autonomy or volition of adherents of these groups. As expounded upon in numerous ways in this volume, the leadership of these groups employ the heretical doctrines and indoctrinations to accomplish this thoroughly demonic purpose. In sum, "absolute submission" of the followers is the ultimate goal, and "absolute authority" of the leadership is the primary premise through which it is effected. The end result is that members gradually yield their innate right of self-governance to their spiritual masters. Again, as previously described in this book, congregants are relentlessly indoctrinated with teaching that they are simply not capable of making their own decisions regarding important and even mundane matters of life, but rather that they should seek the approval, commonly referred to as "witness," of their leader(s) concerning those matters.

11. Systematic Subjugation.

In these groups a performance-based approval and promotion system of members predicated on "proven" loyalty to the leadership is employed as a means of systematic subjugation of congregants. The multilevel leadership hierarchy for these groups is comprised almost entirely of internally "raised up" sub-leaders hand-picked by the senior leadership based on their demonstrated loyalty to the ultimate leader and their acceptance of the adopted authoritarian doctrines and methodologies rather than on the basis of their leadership skills, spiritual acumen, and anointing and appointing by God. In other words, the sub-leaders are almost invariably laymen rather than those with

Fivefold ministry giftings and anointing from God. In essence they are humanly appointed rather than God-appointed, and so rather than being the representatives, surrogates, and spokesmen of God, they are basically the cronies, underbosses, or deputies of the senior leadership.

Loyalty to the leadership is a constant theme at all levels of the culture of these groups. Members are required to sign covenant agreements pledging allegiance and financial support to the leadership and the ministry, and another level of covenant is required of sub-leaders as they progress through the various aspects of the process for being "raised up" as a leader within the group.

Cunning leaders exploit the selfish-ambition of members who desire ascendancy and authority over fellows by dangling in front of them the carrot of prospective leadership appointment and advancement. The members are told that if they are willing to be "broken" and "learn submission" by following the group's particular "leadership training program" — a carefully crafted process fraught with various forms of degradation designed to subjugate and effect "absolute submission" through debasement and indoctrination — then they will be considered as candidates for appointment to various subordinate leadership positions within the church or group, such as a cell or care or task group leader, or deacon. Typically, these degradations consist of the performance of menial tasks such as cleaning toilets and the church facilities, landscaping work, setting up chairs, running errands, acting as the leader's personal valet or servant, and so forth. They are viewed as a perfectly legitimate means for "humbling" and "breaking" the leadership candidate and for "testing" and monitoring their "loyalty," "submission," and "yieldedness."

The more guileful autocrats institute into the culture of the group various psychological personal abasement techniques aimed at further subordinating, or "humbling," as they call it, followers. One of those techniques is a kind of *confidence suppression method* in which the manifest God-given talents, abilities, giftings, callings, and anointings of adherents are deliberately squelched, squashed, and not recognized. For example, someone who has a bona fide gift in music and desires to be used by God in their gifting, would be told that being used in their gift or talent is not nearly as important as them "learning to be obedient and submitted to leadership." So before they could be used in the group, they would have to be willing to set up chairs or clean toilets for a while to gauge and prove their "obedience" (read that *obesience*). Then, if they pass that test, they might be considered for being allowed to participate in the music program of the church at some entry-level position, for example.

All such tactics and techniques, no matter how "sanctified" they may appear in a church setting, are nothing more than classic forms of religious indoctrination and brainwashing so identified in every book or white paper in existence on the topic of psychological persuasion, coercion, and mind control techniques.

12. Excessive Church Discipline.
As we have been discussing throughout this book, in churches and ministries where these fallacious authoritarian doctrines are espoused and the attendant practices employed, abuse and misuse of authority in personal dealings with members is pervasive within the group. Another element of that authoritarian excess is abuse, misuse, and inordinate incidence of

"church discipline." Members who do not toe the line and indiscriminately submit to every dictum and dictate of the leadership downline are "called on the carpet" and summoned to appear before some leader in the chain of leaders to give account and be "dressed down" for their rebellious attitudes and actions. This is all done under the supposedly sanctifying and justifying guise of "church discipline." Of course, church discipline is a scriptural matter, but scripture indicates that it is only to be resorted to as a *last resort* measure in the case of the most egregious cases of overt and continued true *spiritual* offense by leaders or laymen, not as a means of squelching critical thinking, dissent, and criticism, or as a mechanism of mind control and manipulation for the purposes of subjugation and suppression.

Word of Caution and Warning

Having delineated these techniques of unauthorized control and coercion and mechanisms of manipulation, a word of caution and warning is in order in regard to their application.

First, as a caution, please understand that the existence and employment of a few of these techniques and mechanisms within a group does not necessarily mean that the group employing them is a bona fide cult or even a "Discipleship/Shepherding" group. It is not uncommon for people to be totally unaware that certain aspects or subtle nuances of the teaching they espouse and practices they employ are actually erroneous and improper. In some cases, leaders and adherents of aberrant doctrines truly are "sincerely deceived," and are willing to receive reproof, repent, and make appropriate changes, once they are made aware of their error.

Second, strong warning is given against misuse of what is written here as "ammunition" for a mean-spirited, malicious attack against individuals or groups who may be adherents of these authoritarian doctrines for the purposes of discrediting, disparaging, defaming, or harming them in some way. People who engage in this kind of "murdering of your brother" without bathing the situation in prayer, willingness to forgive, and agape-love, and without having restoration through repentance as the objective of reproof, are themselves *wrong*, regardless of how *right* they may be about having detected or discerned error in those they have examined. How unequivocally *wrong* any of us are capable of being in *attitude* and corresponding *actions*, though irrefutably *right* in *assessment*!

* * * *

Important Reminder: This booklet is adapted from Dr. Lambert's book, *Charismatic Captivation, Authoritarian Abuse & Psychological Enslavement in Neo-Pentecostal Churches*, which contains a wealth of information regarding the prevalent problem of hyper-authoritarianism in Neo-Pentecostal churches, how it began, why it is improper, and how to recognize and be set free from it. Readers are strongly encouraged to obtain a copy of that book for a more detailed account of this alarmingly widespread and extremely harmful problem. The book contains much more vital information than what is contained in this booklet, including *The 15 Rs of Recovery from Authoritarian Abuse*, which victims of authoritarian abuse must understand in order to receive real deliverance and true healing from the ravages and trauma of spiritual abuse. A synopsis and ordering information appear in the back of this volume; that plus sample chapters and excerpts are available on the website at: http://www.charismatic-captivation.com.

Charismatic Captivation

Charismatic Captivation, by Dr. Steven Lambert, is the book from which this booklet is adapted. This booklet was published in response to readers' requests for a condensed version they could give to friends and loved ones who were unaware victims of authoritarian abuse. Only a small portion of the wealth of information contained in the book is in this booklet. Thus, we strongly recommend potential spiritual abuse victims read the "big book." The following is some of its contents.

- Introduction to the hyper-authoritarian doctrines, practices, and governmental structures that are accepted and instituted by many Neo-Pentecostal churches, groups, denominations, and networks today, plus Biblical analysis showing why they are irrefutably:
    - unscriptural and thus patently false "doctrines of demons" by which many have been indoctrinated and duped;
    - illegitimate and unauthorized by God;
    - a subtle, but sophisticated scheme of religious enslavement;
    - in actuality, witchcraft/sorcery, cultic and occult;
    - idolatry and spiritual adultery;
    - masked mechanisms for private kingdom-building.
- The history of how these teachings and practices were introduced and infused into the very fabric, foundation, and functions of the Neo-Pentecostal Church, the firestorm of controversy they produced, identification of the leaders who propagated the teachings, the disrepute into which they fell, and their present status.
- How these doctrines/practices are identical to those of a first century Christian cult whose deeds and doctrines Jesus Himself explicitly condemned and denounced in the Bible.
- *The Signs of* Authoritarian *Abuse &* Common *Control Mechanisms* used by self-aggrandizing leaders to captivate and control followers.
- *The 15 R's of Recovery from Authoritarian Abuse* —Biblical steps victims must take to recover from the psychologically traumatizing and spiritually debilitating effects of authoritarian abuse.

To order or read more about *Charismatic Captivation* online, go to: http://www.charismatic-captivation.com.

About The Author

Dr. Steven Lambert has been ordained and ministering the Gospel of Jesus Christ since 1976, serving as a pastor, evangelist, prophet, teacher, speaker, writer/editor, Christian counselor, and media/legal expert on spiritual abuse. He is a Certified Christian Counselor, and holds several earned theological degrees, including a Doctor of Theology and Doctor of Ministry.

He is also the founder of *Ephesians Four Network*, an international fellowship of Fivefold Ministers relating and colaboring for common purposes (*http://www.ephesiansfour.net*).

Dr. Lambert is the author of a number of books, booklets, Bible college courses, and other teaching materials, as well as publisher of an online e-zine: *Spirit Life Magazine,* which is dedicated to extolling, elucidating, and experiencing Life in the Spirit (*http://www.spiritlifemag.com*). His other books include:

- *Charismatic Captivation*
- *The Prophetic Gifts & Office*
- *The Mystery of the Kingdom*
- *Deliverance From Demonic Powers*
- *Dunamis! Power From On High!*

Information regarding these publications is available online at: *http://www.realtruthpublications.com*.

Dr. Lambert travels internationally as a guest speaker on the topic of authoritarian abuse and many other vital prophetic topics. His bio and contact and scheduling information are available on the ministry website at: *http://www.slm.org*. Booking inquiries may be emailed to: *booking@slm.org*.

www.ingramcontent.com/pod-product-compliance
Lightning Source LLC
Chambersburg PA
CBHW061248040426
42444CB00010B/2304